Letters From Venice

Also by Campbell Kay

Play
Phoenix Rising: D. H. Lawrence - Son and Lover (The Phoenix Press)

Poetry
Graffiti In a Narrow Room (Aquila/The Phaeton Press)
The Waste Remains (Aquila/The Phaeton Press)
Devils' Wine (The Phoenix Press)

Stage Adaptation
Cranford (The Phoenix Press)

Recording
Phoenix Rising: D. H. Lawrence - Son and Lover Performed by Paul Slack.
Directed by John Tams. (A.D.A Recording ADA114).

Film
Inside The Mind Of Mr. D. H. Lawrence. Directed by Amand Attar.

Visit www.campbellkay.com

Letters From Venice

New Poems
by
Campbell Kay

The Phoenix Press

First published by The Phoenix Press 2021
© Campbell Kay 2021

ISBN 978-0-9566308-3-4

Published by: The Phoenix Press
                Nottingham Arts Theatre Ltd,
                George Street,
                Nottingham,
                NG1 3BE

Printed and bound in Great Britain by:
Instaprint, 115, Huntingdon Street, Nottingham, NG1 3NF

Publication formatted by Michael Pearson.
Cover illustration: Canal Scene, Venice attributed to Edward Pritchett (1829 - 1864) by kind permission of Dr Alan Thacker.
Back cover photograph courtesy of Andrew Wyles.

All profits from this publication go to Nottingham Arts Theatre, a not for profit educational charity. Registered Charity Number: 1085862

This publication is dedicated to my good friends Ray and Andrew, with pleasant memories of being a best man at their wedding; to David and Alan, my lockdown bubble; and with grateful thanks for my seventieth year to heaven.

CONTENTS

Love And Loss

I

Knowing you are far from here,
Love taunts me with an old desire.
Tonight the darkness and the stars,
As distant from me as you are,
Conspire to mock the love I've lost
And scorn my longing for the past.

II

Thoughts I dare not think, they speak,
While I ... stutter ... inarticulate.
The faltering silence of my voice
Conveys scant meaning; sense avoids.
Broken words dissolve in syllables
Making my poor pleas inaudible.

III

A beggar, not for coin but love,
No alms will ever be enough
To assuage the loneliness of loss;
Of knowing what cannot be; but was.
Love does not fade with he who goes
But with the one who waits and hopes.

The Gamble

I

Lovers and gamblers play
to win though they may
hold a loser's hand. Beginner's
luck I'll beg of love and
play my cards the best I can.

II

Love is a gamble worth the risk,
uncertain though the outcome
proves. It is a lottery, game
or chance; and luck
might favour he who loves.

III

The wheel of love spins on
and on; some other finds
his fortune there. Yet I'll stake
all I have to stake and
hazard hope to win despair.

The Tempest

I

Cruel eastern winds, with
icy ease reviving ancient
enmities, incite the seething,
snarling seas. The tempest's
rage - a hungry roar - devours
the stark and startled shore.

II

Inland the storm's chaotic
clamour dwindles to a distant
murmur and trees, no longer
laden with leaves, shiver in
the winter breeze.
                    Suddenly
the sullen sun drops dimly
from the careless sky; its dull,
diminishing light dissolving
to darkness and the night.

III

The surly storm and winds
remain. Capricious as a
courtesan, the sallow sun
deserts the dawn; while my
poor passion coldly sleeps be-
tween a lonely lover's sheets.

Love In Time Of Strife

(St. Valentine's Day 2017)

Loving boys from heights are hurled,
Their bodies shattered as their world;
And shrapnel, like confetti strewn,
Destroys the bride and her young groom;
While children bloodied, bowed, bereft,
Paint pictures of the lives they've left:
No parents now to praise their art,
Strafe bombing tears their kin apart.

Let us, on this sweet martyr's day,
Incline our heads remembering they
Whose lives so cruelly have been lost
To conflicts present, yet and past.
Love is the best of us and love remains
No matter how the world may change.

In Hagia Sophia

I

The sunlit dome
of wisdom and
of holiness -
sacred with
solemn majesty -
lets the light
of holy wisdom
illumine life's
dark mystery.

II

Beneath prayer mats,
the marbled floor
floes out - a vast
and ice-bound sea;
while we,
two mortals,
walk on water
blessed by
love's divinity.

Note
Early Christian pilgrims to the, then, church of Santa Sofia were awestruck
by the white marble floor which, with its ripple-like grey bands, was
frequently compared to an expanse of frozen water.

Now

There is no yesterday, nor tomorrow,
Only today for ... joy ... or sorrow.
It was so ten thousand years ago
And will be in ten thousand more.
For now is the past and future too
And all the splendour of loving you
In the present is a gift of time;
If only you will now be mine.

Petrarch for Laura pined in vain.
In sestet, sonnet and quatrain,
He hymned his love but was denied
From first sight until Laura died.
Let us not vainly love but vow
To seize the potency of now.

Time Past And Passing

I

Clocks have never been my friends.
Their faces, white as innocence,
Belie the guile of petty thieves
That double deal our paltry years,
Stealing whatever joys we have,
Bequeathing us a loveless grave.

II

Clocks' hands point out the time we lack,
Moving ever forward, never back.
Relentless hours and minutes mass
While months and years, like seconds, pass;
And we must go, while time remains,
An hourglass counting its own grains.

III

Clocks' voices tick on endlessly,
The soundtrack of our mortality.
We have not world enough this time,
I hear the midnight's darkling chime.
Let us, with one immortal kiss,
Silence the clocks' insidious ticks.

Lost In Love

Though some time I have longed for you,
And you still unaware,
I have not found the courage yet
To tell you that I care.

A beggar sooner might entreat
A boon from passers-by,
Than I could utter my poor plea -
So lost in love am I.

Will you love or won't you, love?
Such questions still remain.
Better I should silent stay
Than speak my love in vain.

The Lover's Complaint

All day I mourn, all night I yearn
For you to love me in return.
Vast argosies of tears and sighs
I've ventured just to gain that prize.

Dull days melt slowly into night
And loving is a sour delight.
A watchful clock, I tell each hour;
Till life and love seem mine no more.

What a wealth of wit and lies
Have I spent on this enterprise;
And we two scarce more amorous
Than corpses in a charnel house.

The darkness dazzles, and grows less,
Night thoughts dissolved to emptiness;
And all my useless, spent desires
The ghostly echoes of goodbyes.

Things Fall Apart

The tarnished moon
can scarce recall
she holds tides and
madmen in her thrall.

The wayward hawk,
its gyves undone,
reels headlong towards
the melting sun.

And I, lone dancer
on the shore,
must dance, and dance,
and so implore

For one to join me
in the dance;
for another's footprints
on the sands.

Phantasmagoria

I trudge across the lonely heath
While wintry weather, chill as death,
Makes ghosts of every laboured breath.

The cottage of our summer days
Is shrouded in a pallid haze;
Neglect and ruin haunt the place.

The cruel wind winnows furze and gorse.
Ice stops the river in its course.
On the bridge, a phantom of remorse,

I stand and contemplate the past:
The summer love that could not last
Nor survive the ghostly winter's blast.

And desire, that once was overwhelming,
Flickers - an ember's fitful burning -
Sad spectre of our youthful yearning.

Note to a Friend

The house is empty
without you there.
I cough, and breathe
the dusty air;
disturbing each dark
and lonely space,
like a strange
and uninvited guest.

No longer easy
in my mind,
I try to make
some new design;
to shape the darkness
and the dust
with which my random
life seems cursed.

But no page of words
will ever explain
the hollow darkness
in my brain;
nor why I linger
on the stair
with other ghosts
who are not here.

In His Cups

An hour before the raucous sun
Announces that the day's begun,
I drown whatever dregs are left
And follow the sottish stars to bed.

I've drunk your health ten thousandfold
And an empty glass was my reward.
A headstrong minion of the moon,
You stole my love and left me none.

I stand, as one at an abyss,
Peering in to the emptiness,
The void of your indifference.

The grave, quiet witness of my hurt,
Pities the wretch that you desert
And welcomes me to her cold heart.

The Tryst

The sly moon creeps
across the sky, illumining
the night's dark
course with slivers
of its silver light, chill
as logical discourse.

The boy yawns wearily,
and stares, while I return
his sullen greeting.
This is no place for us
to talk. Custom and boredom
frustrate our meeting.

That we should part is
obvious. But neither of us says
it's so. Indecision has
betrayed us both. And, though
we feel the moon's dark pull,
we neither of us want to go.

The Meeting

Pride, and
the lateness of the hour,
made me desert
our meeting place;

yet still
I wonder, foolishly,
if perhaps he came
and waits for me.

The Spiders

The dancer,
like a hang-
ing man,
will twist
and turn upon
the air;

while I must
spread some
paper out
and comb the
spiders from
my hair.

The spiders
brood upon
the page,
dark spinners
in their
silent web,

stitching
the fabric
of my thought
with fragile
and quick-
silver thread.

Breaking Silence

Breaking
silence, like breaking
ice, takes
courage and a steady hand.

Suspended
in the frozen space
between
one silence and the next,

Words wait,
like dumbstruck fish,
to land, cold
and wriggling, on the page.

Another Madness

When once
the mad boy
in his passion,
with acid
and with
naked tears,

destroys
the darkest
memory of
his lunatic
and crazy
years;

he'll walk
imagination's
tight-rope,
above the
knives and
burning coals,

till his mind
becomes both
dunce and
demon - a mad
miscellany
of fools.

The Hawk Adrift

His mind was
like a rusty axe
carving shadows
out of air,

which merged
and melted into
space, falling like
a bird on fire;

and the hawk,
adrift upon the wind,
plunged downward
at the water's edge

to where the
bones of seaweed
lay under the grey
and guilty sky.

Silence And The Poet

Blind, with drunkenness
   and rage,
locked in his body's
   mocking cage,

he seeks for words that
   might explain
the gathering silence
   in his brain.

But drink and anger have
   combined
to blur the edges of
   his mind;

and words no longer can
   be found
to translate image
   into sound.

Waiting For The End

Trapped
inside his ancient
skin, death bored
him and his eyes
grew dim; his grudging
breaths, like ghosts
in ice, were heavy
as the sound
of sighs.

Each day
his mind was dull and
lost, like windows
scarred by morning
frost; and cold blood
trickled through his
veins, grown tired
of waiting for
the end.

She Refuses To Mourn

Love promised more than she expected,
Delivered less than she desired.
Like birth, it was a gift unasked for,
Asked for by the one who gave.

Her lover, like an ardent hearse,
Mechanical and slick as death,
Brought satisfaction of a kind
And of his kind was satisfied.

Such vanities of blood and bone
Are grief enough to heap on graves.
They suffer most who will not mourn,
She would not mourn who suffered most.

The Visitor

There is no light shines on the dead
But shows the living what to dread
When we are brought to death's estate;

No tour of ancient monument,
Or sepulchre in shrouded light,
But proves to those who enter there
That there awaits eternal night
Wherein each man must meet his fate;

And so we stumble from the crypt
In which our darkest fears are kept
Desirous that our death should wait.

If history were possessed of truth,
And we could comprehend the past,
The mystery of death's embrace
Unlocked from every burial cask,
Is knowledge that would come too late;

For, even as we realise
The simple truth of man's demise,
Death knocks and enters at our gate.

The Vulture

A comic undertaker's
mute, clad in a
shabby, threadbare suit,

he sat, like one who
prays in church,
head bowed upon his
blackened perch.

Though captive,
he could not
disguise
the chill indifference
of his eyes.

Remorse would never force
apart the charnel
house that was his heart;

nor free once more
those dying things
who lost all hope
beneath his wings.

The Horseman's Return

I

The stones cough
up their secret
blood; the raven's
voice is hoarse
again; the enemy
lie dead or dying,
life spilling from
their ragged throats.

II

Lamentation rends
the air like thunder;
sad women search
among the slain;
the horseman rides
into the distance,
blood glinting on
his tarnished spear.

III

The threadbare sun
deserts the sky;
a hunched owl in
the courtyard screams;
the horseman will
return to find
the spoils of war
are blood and tears.

The Conversation

death in
his cradle
cursed
     the sun

and whispered
in young
     adam's ear

awakened by
their secrecy
the serpent
       listened
in the shade

but hearing
that they
spoke
     of love

he smiled and
fell
   asleep again

A Beginning

i

the kiss
    of maker
        and of maggot
from dust
and clay
        created man

and gazing in his
        crystal
        skull
man saw the void
of future / past

the curse
        of maggot
        and of maker
from earth
and ash
        created death

and god the serpent
        in his
        frenzy
bit the cord that
held man fast

ii

two
    paces
from the garden
man wept and
dreamed of love
while maiden veiled
in sorrow desired
her gentle lord

but man a dragon
in his passion
ignored her tender
words and cursed
the first maiden
with a belly
full of
    god

Charnel Knowledge

I

When
the spider
wove god's epitaph,

men's
eyes were
diamonds in the dust;

and garlands
withered
on the grave,

like blossoms
in a desert place.

II

Pale
as moon -
light on a skull,

or skin
stretched
tight across the bone,

the dead man
rubbed his
eyes and woke

to taste the
maggot on his tongue.

Variation

the dancer,
           stumb
                 ling
in his frenzy,

saw the prophet's
                 severed
head
       (smiling
       like an
       open scar)

reflected
on the silver plate;

and the eyes
of the prophet
were opening
             slowly

                    (like nostrils
                    sniffing a
                    rotting skull)

till they stared
at the dancer;

lidless and holy;

weeping,
         like a guilty god.

The Scare-crow Man

I

when god
betrayed
the serpent sun

his voice
as dry as
powdered glass

breathed
life into
the sleeping dust;

created
then the
scare-crow man

and clothed
him in his
ragged flesh.

II

the scare-crow
   man, with eyes
      of blood, wept

acid on his thorny
   bed, while in the
      east the serpent

sun shone black
   and silent as his
      tongue filling
the air with soundless screams.

III

once louder than
the crested cock
that crows the
morning bright awake;

twice crueller than
the hammer thud
that gave the wood
and metal shape;

the scare-crow man
again denied
his trinity with
god and snake.

Lost Love

Those birds that haunt
their prey by night,
in the tall trees preen
their tattered feathers;
while the blind moon
staggers through the sky,
winking at their
midnight terrors.

You can feel the tremor
of their wings, when the moon
is reeling from its course;
and we have nothing left
to lose but the shadow
of a love that's lost.

Who Lie With Shadows

I

Dull candles flicker,
pale as ghosts that serve
to usher daylight hence,
their guttering silence
fills the room, familiar
as the talk of friends.

II

My arms might reach you
in the darkness, your body
veiled and ill-defined,
for memory, as cruel as
moonlight, casts strange
shadows on the mind.

III

If there were substance
to the darkness, I'd hold
you, sinister and bright,
but those who choose to lie
with shadows are lonely
as the ghosts of night.

The Edge Of Night

I

At the edge of night
    where day begins,
time's garments all
    are strewn in rags;

and, naked as the hours
    that pass, the spider,
aping death, will weave,
    from silken thread,

love's winding sheet.

II

And, waking from
    this tomb of sleep,
the man, new-risen
    at his side, will

shower the lordly
    boy with pearls; till
willow-like, his
    body curves beneath

affection's tender weight.

Hunger

a serpent
   coils around
      the heart as
greedily
      we share
         the dark

two strangers
   sprawled upon
      a bed our bodies
streaked
      with tears
         and sweat

for hunger
   will not cease
      to prowl till
love
      makes victims
         of us all

The Wound

When all
is sour
or broken and spilled,
the tear-
stained
night attempts to heal.

Caressed
by salt,
and bathed with tears,
the wound
is deeper
than the scars.

And, in
the tear-
kissed afternoon,
the scars
may heal
but not the wound.

Mirrors

I

When I look
in a mirror
there can
be no mistake
that familiar
reflection
must be my face.

I rely on
a mirror
to always
reflect
the image
which I
have come
to expect;

fearing
the day I
might see
in its place
the startled
reflection of
some other face.

II

Our trust
in mirrors
is misplaced.

They make us
all appear
two-faced.

Vanity

Those boys, who once adorned my youth,
Were often spendthrift with the truth;
And I could never get enough
Of their falsehoods or their love.

But now those truant days are past,
My heart has learned this truth at last:
Such passion is not all it seems
And we grow older than our dreams.

I choose my lovers with more care,
They're fatter now and have less hair.
Old men must learn humility
For age affords no vanity.

Letters from Venice

I

Between the raven and the fox
much talk of boys and sin
and of the pleasures boys can bring.

Throughout the winter Corvo penned
letters to his wealthy friend.

II

Venice, 20th Jan., 1913

Dear Masson Fox,
                    I've found the boy,
In byways dark where pleasures cloy,
Where all the vices Christians fear are
Bought and sold for thirty lira.

A boy, whose praises should be sung
In Plato's Greek or Martial's Latin,
Whose slender limbs are firm and strong,
Clothed in skin as smooth as satin.

A boy, whose beauty blinds the sun,
Whose eyes will make the stars look tame,
Whose tender lips, surpassed by none,
Are meant for pleasure not for shame.

Yet these poor words can ne ' er express
This paragon of boyhood's loveliness.
Perhaps, in the photographs, you will find
That beauty which stirs heart and mind.

Last night I slept in a leaky sandolo,
I have no money for wine or tobacco.
It would profit us much if, perchance, you'd send
Some pelf to cover our expenses.

Frdk. Rolfe
(Your affectionate friend)

III

Poor cunning Corvo, if you thought
the wily Fox would ever send
pelf to purchase nameless sin.

Winter is cruel, not least in Venice,
he promised pounds but proffered pennies.

Notes
Frederick Rolfe (1860 - 1913), the self-styled Baron Corvo (Italian for
crow or raven), was an eccentric English writer who spent his latter years
in penury in Venice.
Charles Masson Fox (1866 - 1935) was a well-to-do Cornish timber
merchant and shipping magnate who shared some of Rolfe's proclivities.
The photographs, presumably taken by the German photographer
Wilhelm von Gloeden (1856 - 1931). Another self-styled baron, von
Gloeden was famous for his nude studies of Sicilian boys whom he
photographed during a stay of many years in Taormina.
Sandolo, a smaller, less ornate and less stable version of a gondola.
Pelf, archaic slang, money earned from dubious sources often to be spent
on dubious endeavours.

A Winter's Tale

I

The sexton's horny-handled spade
Digs divots from the waiting grave;
While watchful toads and ravens curse
Plumed horses, tethered to the hearse,
Whose muffled hooves on frozen ground
A melancholy tattoo sound.

Now some few mourners shuffle past,
Hats in hands, and eyes downcast,
To hear the parson's voice insist
That we are ashes, earth and dust.

And grief they feel, and passion too,
More sharp than any parson knows.
For who can tell if nettles strewn
Will wither sooner than the rose;
Or whether rose and petals fell
A love to hide or to reveal.

II

In azure meadows harebells ring
Loud carillons to welcome Spring
And lenten lilies herald forth
The season's plenitudinous growth.

A myriad mornings we will rise
From slumber and sweet reveries;
While wanton boys, still half asleep,
Yawn promises they will not keep.

But we, who have lost more than most,
Know better than to mourn the past.
Think then of all that we would gain
If we should dare to love again:

A love, new-bidden by the word,
A love not hidden from the world.

Acknowledgements

It goes without saying that, apart from the author, several people work towards the publication of a book.

Therefore, I would like to offer my warmest thanks to a number of friends and staff at The Phoenix Press, who have contributed to bringing **Letters From Venice** to publication.

My particular gratitude goes to the following:
Gilly Brown for her friendship and encouragement;
Sue Mellor for her advice and critical appreciation;
Michael Pearson for his attention to detail and infinite patience;
and Martin Vickers for his accuracy in proofreading the volume.

However, any errors, which may have crept into the volume, I acknowledge mine.